J 954.065
Green
Green, Jen

Gandhi and the Quit India Movement

DAYS OF DECISION

Gandhi and the Quit India Movement

Heinemann
LIBRARY
Chicago, Illinois

Jen Green

Visit our web site at www.heinemannraintree.com

Edited by Andrew Farrow, Adrian Vigliano, and Mark
Friedman
Designed by Cynthia Della-Rovere
Original illustrations © Capstone Global Library Ltd.
Illustrated by H L Studios and Cynthia Della-Rovere
Picture research by Elizabeth Alexander
Production by Sophia Argyris

Originated by Capstone Global Library Ltd
Printed in China by RR Donnelley South China

17 16 15 14 13
10 9 8 7 6 5 4 3 2 1

Library of Congress Cataloging-in-Publication Data
Green, Jen.

Gandhi and the Quit India movement / Jen Green.

pages cm—(Days of decision)

Includes bibliographical references and index.

ISBN 978-1-4329-7635-4 (hb)—ISBN 978-1-4329-7642-2
(pb) 1. Gandhi, Mahatma, 1869-1948—Juvenile literature.
2. Gandhi, Mahatma, 1869-1948—Political and social
views—Juvenile literature. 3. India—History—Quit India
movement, 1942—Juvenile literature. I. Title.

DS481.G3G725 2013

954.03'5092—dc23   2012041681

Acknowledgments
The author and publishers are grateful to the following
for permission to reproduce copyright material: Alamy
p. 37 (©Dinodia Photos); Corbis pp. 13 (©Bettmann),
15 (©Hulton-Deutsch Collection), 23 (©Bettmann), 25
(©Underwood & Underwood), 49 (©Bettmann); Gamma-
Keystone via Getty Images pp. 17, 24, 41, imprint page
(Keystone-France); Getty Images pp. 8, 19 (Hulton Archive),
28 (FPG), 31 (Dinodia Photos/Hulton Archive), 43, 51
(Keystone/Hulton Archive), 47 (Margaret Bourke-White/Time
& Life Pictures), 52 (STR/AFP); Photoshot p. 21t (©UPPA);
Press Association Images pp. 5, 35 (Preston Grover/AP), 21b
(Max Desfor/AP), 22 (PA Archive), 33, 38, 39 (AP); Topfoto
pp. 11, 14, 27 (Dinodia).

Background and design features reproduced with the
permission of Shutterstock (©Picsfive, ©Petrov Stanislav,
©Zastolskiy Victor, ©design36, ©a454).

Cover photograph of Mahatma Gandhi on the steps of 10
Downing Street, 1931 reproduced with the permission
of Superstock (Science and Society); Cover photograph
of a demonstration in Bombay City reproduced with the
permission of Corbis (©Hulton-Deutsch Collection).

We would like to thank Benjamin M. Zachariah for his
invaluable help in the preparation of this book.

Every effort has been made to contact copyright holders of
any material reproduced in this book. Any omissions will
be rectified in subsequent printings if notice is given to the
publisher.

Contents

Some words are printed in **bold**, like this. You can find out what they mean by looking in the glossary on page 59.

An Arrest in Bombay

It is just before dawn on Malabar Hill, a wealthy suburb of the great port of Bombay (now called Mumbai), India. The date is August 9, 1942—almost midway through World War II (1939–1945). The heat is oppressive even at this hour. Only a few people are out and about to witness the sudden uproar as a group of police cars heads up the street. The cars screech to a halt outside an imposing dwelling called Birla House. Policemen swarm out of the cars and knock loudly on the door with their wooden batons. After a short while, the door opens and the police pour inside.[1]

What is going on? The Indian politician Mohandas Gandhi is staying in the house. Gandhi is a leader of the **Indian National Congress (INC)**. This is a political party that has been campaigning for Indian independence from the United Kingdom for many years. (India has been ruled by the United Kingdom since 1858.) Now an old man of 73, Gandhi is one of the **British Empire's** most outspoken critics.

Gandhi's most recent criticism is about India's role in World War II. In 1939, the United Kingdom declared war on Germany. It announced that India, part of its empire, was also at war—but Indian leaders were not consulted. Since then, India's contribution to the war has been huge. As a believer in nonviolence, Gandhi has been firmly against India's involvement in the war. Instead, he has launched a campaign called Quit India, calling on the British to leave India immediately and grant India its independence.

In the thick of war

World War II began in 1939. In 1941, the war became a truly global conflict, as German forces invaded the **Soviet Union**. Japan had entered the war on the side of Germany, and soon after mounted an attack on the U.S. naval fleet in Pearl Harbor, Hawaii. This brought the United States into the war on the side of the Allies, which included the United Kingdom, its empire, and the Soviet Union.

In August 1942—the time of Gandhi's arrest at Birla House—the war raged throughout the Pacific. The UK **colony** of Burma, east of India, had recently fallen to the Japanese, who were threatening India's eastern borders. The conquest of India seemed like a real possibility.[2]

Call for rebellion

An INC meeting has taken place in Bombay over the last few days. Before a crowd of thousands of people, the Indian National Congress has declared its unanimous support for Gandhi's Quit India campaign. Gandhi called upon the United Kingdom to transfer power to Indian leaders immediately— or face a nonviolent rebellion against UK rule on a massive scale. The scene that is now unfolding on Malabar Hill is the UK response to this. The UK government feels that in a time of war, it has no choice but to stamp down on the protest and arrest Gandhi at Birla House.

Crackdown

Now the small crowd that has gathered outside the house watches as police escort the frail, shaven-headed leader to the waiting car and on to prison. Other INC leaders are also arrested in dawn raids.

Gandhi (seated) and fellow leaders address a political meeting in the 1940s.

The arrests will not go unchallenged. All over India, the news will spark waves of protest. But not all of the protests will be nonviolent, as Gandhi urges them to be. The UK response will also be violent.

Over the next years, Gandhi's Quit India campaign will have far-reaching consequences for all of India. It will affect the politics of the whole region, and its people, right up to the present day. Gandhi's campaign will indeed prove very important—but not in the way he had planned.

India Under the Raj

By 1942, when Gandhi launched his Quit India campaign, the British Empire's influence in India had existed for hundreds of years. European interest in the region began back in the 1500s.

In the 1500s, **Muslim** emperors called the Mughals ruled India. By the 1600s, Britain, France, and Portugal had set up trading posts and built forts around India's coasts. A trading company called the British East India Company represented the interests of the British Empire. It gradually grew more powerful as the influence of the Mughals declined in the 1700s and as the many small states that made up India became more independent.[1]

In the early days, Britain's chief interest in India was trade, not conquest (taking over the country). However, the East India Company gradually came to collect taxes from Indian landowners, and later it collected taxes more widely, using force when taxes were withheld. In 1757, Robert Clive of the East India Company defeated the ruler of Bengal, in eastern India. Many historians see this as the start of the British Empire in India.[2]

Rebellion and the Raj

By the early 1800s, the United Kingdom was the dominant European power in the region. The East India Company continued to increase the size of its lands and influence. But in 1857, UK interests received a setback. A rebellion started among Indian soldiers called sepoys. They refused to obey an order to use gun cartridges that they believed were greased with beef and pork fat. This was contrary to the beliefs of India's two main religions, Hinduism (the religion of **Hindus**) and Islam (the religion of Muslims).

The soldiers' rebellion began near the city of Delhi and quickly spread across north-central India. It took the United Kingdom a year to stop it. The UK government

The subcontinent

The British referred to India as "the **subcontinent**." The region included what is now Pakistan in the northwest, Bangladesh in the east, and also neighboring Burma. In 1900, this vast region held about 292 million people, who belonged to different cultures and had different religious beliefs. Roughly 70 percent of the population were Hindus and 25 percent were Muslims. There were also Christians, **Sikhs**, Buddhists, and Jains.[3] Many different languages were spoken throughout India.

now decided to take direct control of India. The lands of the East India Company became **British India**. The UK administration was called the **Raj**, a **Hindi** word meaning "rule."

The United Kingdom controlled about two-thirds of India directly. British India was divided into 11 provinces, each of which was ruled by a governor. These governors reported to the UK monarch's (queen's) representative in India, called the **viceroy**. The remaining third of India was made up of over 550 independent **princely states** of varying sizes, each with its own prince. However, most princes cooperated with the United Kingdom.

In 1876, the UK **Parliament** gave the UK queen, Victoria, a new title: she became Empress of India, to reflect the United Kingdom's control over the country. During the late 1800s, the United Kingdom's army in India (mainly made up of Indian soldiers commanded by senior officers from the United Kingdom) campaigned in neighboring Afghanistan and Burma, bringing more land under UK control. The British saw India as the "jewel in the crown" of the British Empire, which was by then the largest empire in the world.

Key
- British rule
- Indian states
- --·-- Modern boundary

Kashmir
Delhi
Baluchistan
Rajputana
Calcutta
Bombay
Hyderabad
BURMA
Mysore
N
Travancore
CEYLON

This map shows India under the Raj (British rule) around 1850. Britain controlled about two-thirds of the Indian subcontinent at this time.

Life under the Raj

A large network of people working in **civil service** jobs ran British India. Officials from the United Kingdom brought their families to India and enjoyed a privileged lifestyle there. These white men, called *sahibs*, enjoyed dining in clubs and joining in the occasional tiger hunt.[4] Their wives, called *memsahibs*, ran their households with the aid of numerous servants. There was very little social contact between Indians and most whites. Indians were barred from European clubs, from top civil service jobs, and from becoming army officers.

The British King George V participated in this tiger hunt in India. The white hunters mounted on elephants have killed three tigers.

The United Kingdom's interest in India remained mainly commercial (related to money). The country grew wealthy by exploiting India's natural resources. The British set up tea, coffee, and cotton **plantations** and iron and coal mines in India. They constructed railroads as well as telegraph and (later) telephone lines. These improvements made it easier to **export** Indian resources, such as minerals and food products. India also became a major market for **imported** British manufactured goods, such as glass and textiles. This damaged India's own glass and textile industries.

The British did not spend money on primary education or help India to industrialize.[5] As a result, the vast majority of Indians were uneducated and lived in poverty. But the princely elite—although a minority—were well educated, and some princes were very wealthy.

Birth of the independence movement

Many Indians had resisted UK rule since the days of the East India Company. In 1885, a group of Western-educated Indian lawyers and other professionals founded India's first political party, the Indian National Congress, often referred to as the Congress. At the time, its members mostly did not challenge the United Kingdom's right to rule India. Instead, they debated politics and economics, India's future, and how Indians might achieve higher status under the current system. From the beginning, INC members were mainly Hindu, but they also included Muslims, Sikhs, and people of other faiths. It was not until 1906 that Muslim members of the Indian National Congress broke away to form a separate political party for Muslims, the **All-India Muslim League**.

Birth of Gandhi

Around the time when the Indian National Congress was founded, a young man was growing up in the northwestern Indian state of Gujarat, and he would one day become the party's most famous leader. Mohandas Karamchand Gandhi was born on October 2, 1869, in the small port town of Porbandar. His father, Karamchand, was *diwan*, or **prime minister**, of this tiny, semi-independent state, ruling in the name of the local prince.

The Gandhis were wealthy. Six generations of Gandhis had been *diwans* there.[6] But within India's **caste** system (see the box), the Gandhis were not high ranking. They belonged to the class of Vaishyas, or merchants, and within that, the subclass of Banias, or grocers. (The name Gandhi means "grocer.") However, by the 1800s, the caste system had relaxed a little, and members of the caste of Vaishyas were allowed to enter other professions.

The Hindu caste system

Like 70 percent of all Indians, Gandhi's family was Hindu. Hindu society is traditionally divided into four main tiers called castes, with hundreds of subcastes. Everyone had to stay within the caste he or she was born into. The highest caste, the Brahmins, were traditionally priests. Next came the Kshatriyas, the soldier caste, and the Vaishyas, who were merchants and craftspeople. The fourth tier were the Shudras, made up of farmers and workers. Outside the caste system and considered lower than the Shudras were the **Untouchables**, who did all the worst and dirtiest jobs, such as cleaning toilets.[7]

Early years

Mohandas Gandhi's mother, Putlibai, was his father's fourth wife. Mohandas was her fourth and youngest child. While Mohandas respected his father, he greatly admired his mother. The Gandhis were Hindu, but Putlibai belonged to a small sect (group) that studied **Islamic** texts as well as Hindu scriptures. A devout woman, she **fasted** regularly.

Mohandas spent his early years in a three-story house that his father shared with his brothers and their families. At school, Mohandas did not do well at first. He was a nervous, painfully shy boy. He was also very honest and would not lie, even when a teacher encouraged him to do so. As a boy, Mohandas was drawn to Jainism, an ancient Indian religion with followers who practiced an extreme form of nonviolence toward all living things. This set of beliefs is called *ahimsa*.

Marriage

In 1883, at the age of just 13, Mohandas Gandhi was married to a girl named Kasturbai, who was also 13. Kasturbai was uneducated and could not read or write. Their parents arranged the match. Gandhi became obsessed with Kasturbai. Wildly jealous, he tried to restrict her freedom, but the strong-willed Kasturbai resisted. Gandhi would later speak out against marrying so young.

Gandhi's parents hoped that one of their sons would grow up to be *diwan* like Karamchand. Training as a lawyer was thought to be good preparation for this. So, at 18, Mohandas left India to study law in London, England, leaving behind his wife and a newborn son, Harilal. His devout mother feared he might be corrupted by life in London and adopt Western ways such as drinking alcohol and eating meat. Gandhi vowed not to do this.

Studying religions

In England, several members of the Vegetarian Society were interested in the religions of other cultures. Gandhi began to study religious texts such as the Muslim holy book, the Koran, and the Hindu sacred text, the Bhagavad Gita. He also studied the Christian New Testament. He was particularly impressed by the New Testament's story of the Sermon on the Mount, which describes Jesus Christ preaching a message of nonviolence to a large crowd and urging his followers to "turn the other cheek" if attacked.

Training to be a lawyer

Gandhi arrived in London in the fall of 1888. Eager to fit in with middle-class life there, he bought expensive clothes, including a top hat, and started dancing and elocution (speaking) lessons. His native language was Gujarati (the language of the Gujarat province), and his English was poor. Gandhi was lonely at first, but he eventually found friends when he joined the Vegetarian Society of England.

In 1891, Gandhi gained his qualifications to become a lawyer. He sailed for India just two days later. Upon his arrival, he received the devastating news that his mother had died. (His father had died back in 1885.)

The young man now set out to practice as a lawyer. But he was still so painfully shy that he was unable to speak at his first court case and had to leave the court in shame. Next, his brother Lakshmidas asked him to plead his case with a UK official who had fired him. Gandhi agreed, but the interview went badly and he was thrown out of the official's office.

After this experience, Gandhi felt disillusioned with local politics. When an opportunity to work for an Indian law firm in South Africa came up, he took the job. Gandhi sailed for South Africa, leaving Kasturbai in India with two young sons.

This photo shows Gandhi (bottom right) with members of the Vegetarian Society in England in 1890.

Birth of a Leader

Gandhi arrived in South Africa in the spring of 1893. India and South Africa had one thing in common at the time: they were both largely ruled by Europeans. In South Africa, half a million whites dominated two million Africans.[1] There were two large UK colonies, Natal and Cape Colony, and two **Boer** republics, Transvaal and Orange Free State. The Boers were farmers of Dutch descent. The region was also home to around 75,000 Indians.[2] Many Indians were contracted to work for very low pay on plantations. There were also professionals, like Gandhi.

A turning point

Gandhi's ship docked at Durban, on South Africa's east coast. He traveled by train and then stagecoach to take up his job in Pretoria, in the Transvaal. The young lawyer bought a first-class train ticket, as was his habit, but he was later told that only whites could travel first class. When he argued about this, he was thrown off the train and forced to spend the night on a freezing railroad platform. Later, he continued by stagecoach. During this journey, he was forced to ride outside, and when he refused to sit at the driver's feet, he was beaten. It was a stark introduction to the kind of racism suffered every day by Indians and Africans in South Africa. For Gandhi, this was a turning point. Should he quit his job and go home?

The young lawyer resolved to stay and fight for the rights of Indians in South Africa. After reaching Pretoria, he addressed a meeting of Indians and was surprised to find he had no difficulty speaking in public about something he believed in. He learned about the position of Indians in the Transvaal. They were banned from holding land or voting and forbidden to go out at night. Gandhi urged his

Decisive words: Encountering racism

Reflecting on these early experiences in South Africa, Gandhi later wrote:

"My first contact with British authority in [South Africa] was not of a happy character. I discovered that as a man and as an Indian I had no rights. More correctly, I discovered that I had no rights as a man because I was an Indian."[3]

Gandhi (seated center) surrounded by his staff in his first law firm in Johannesburg, South Africa.

fellow Indians to fight for equality with whites. He also urged the Muslims and Hindus within the community to resolve their differences, in order to be worthy of equality.

Campaigning in Natal

Gandhi finished his legal work quite quickly. He headed back to Durban, in Natal, intending to sail back to India. But in Durban, he learned that the Indians in Natal were about to lose their voting rights. He decided to stay to lead the struggle to keep voting rights. He founded a political party called the Natal Indian Congress, which he modeled on the Indian National Congress back home.

Realizing he would need to be in South Africa for a while, Gandhi sailed to India to fetch his family. On his return to Durban, he was beaten up by a white mob, who had heard of his role in the rights movement. It was a rude introduction for his wife, Kasturbai. She was further shocked when she reached Gandhi's home and discovered his household included "Untouchables," who were traditionally outcast from Hindu society (see page 9). She was also surprised to find her husband living very simply, having given away most of his earnings to the poor. It took some time for Kasturbai to understand and eventually share her husband's views on these issues.

Ambulance Corps

In 1899, war broke out in South Africa between the British and the Boers. While highly critical of the attitudes toward Indians he saw in South Africa, Gandhi still felt loyal to the British Empire. So, he founded an Indian Ambulance Corps, which was made up of 1,100 Indians who helped the British wounded. He also served within the corps, earning a medal. A British journalist who met him in the field described Gandhi as cheerful and kind in the midst of appalling conditions that depressed every other soldier.[4] Gandhi was becoming a leader who inspired love and respect.

India and South Africa

In 1901, Gandhi returned to India. He set up a law firm in Bombay and attended INC meetings. But before long, he received a summons from Indians in the Transvaal, who needed his help. He returned to South Africa and set up a law practice in Johannesburg. He also started a newspaper for the Indian community called *Indian Opinion*.

Truth force

In 1906, the government in the Transvaal introduced a new law that required Indians to register with the authorities, have their fingerprints taken, and carry an identity pass at all times. Since whites did not have to do this, Gandhi saw the new law as racist and unjust.

Gandhi thought deeply and came up with a new form of resistance. He called it **satyagraha**, which means "truth force." This form of resistance required great courage, because it meant protesters had to remain nonviolent, even if the police used force. The aim was not only to change the law, but also to force the opposition to see

Gandhi with fellow members of the Indian Ambulance Corps during the Boer War in South Africa, 1899–1900.

Gandhi and spirituality

In 1904, Gandhi set up a community near Durban called Phoenix Farm. Members of the community grew their own food and lived simple, spiritual lives. Spirituality became increasingly important to Gandhi during this period. In 1906, he took a vow of celibacy (to abstain from sexual relations) to purify and strengthen himself for the trials that lay ahead. Kasturbai supported him in this, perhaps partly because they already had four children by this point.

Gandhi and his wife Kasturbai. Early in their marriage the couple had their differences, but Kasturbai later gave her husband her unwavering support.

the justice of the campaign—in other words, to win the hearts and minds of the enemy.

At a meeting in Johannesburg, thousands of Indians pledged to resist the new law nonviolently. The *satyagraha* campaign was launched. Gandhi was arrested and thrown in jail, but he was then taken to negotiate with the defense minister, Jan Smuts. This was because the protest was so influential that the government felt the need to respond. Eventually, the authorities backed down, and the law was overturned.

In 1910, the Boer states and UK colonies united to form the Union of South Africa. The new government imposed a tax on Indians and refused to recognize Indian marriages. Gandhi led marches and campaigns against the new laws and spent more time in prison. Eventually, the authorities gave in.

In 1914, after 21 years in South Africa, Gandhi felt his work there was done. As his family left for India, Jan Smuts, now the president of South Africa, remarked: "The saint has left our shores, I hope, forever."[5]

Noncooperation

When Gandhi's family arrived in Bombay in January 1915, they found India overshadowed by World War I (1914–1918).

Because India was a colony of the United Kingdom, India became involved in the war when the United Kingdom declared war on Germany in 1914. In return, the United Kingdom had promised some measure of independence for India after the war was over. Indian troops fought in many battles during the war.

In India, INC leaders welcomed Gandhi back. His campaigns in South Africa had been reported in the newspapers. In 1908, he had written a book called *Hind Swaraj*, or *Indian **Home Rule***, in which he called for Indian independence.

There were now two groups within the Indian National Congress. The **nationalists**, led by Bal Gangadhar Tilak, wanted to remove the British from India. Moderates, led by Gopal Krishna Gokhale, were working for reforms under UK rule that would give Indians more power.[1] The Indian National Congress included influential Muslims, although some had left to join the All-India Muslim League (formed in 1906).

Gandhi's book identified him with the nationalists, but the whole Indian National Congress welcomed him. Gokhale advised Gandhi to avoid speaking publicly for a year before taking an

Travels in India

Following Gokhale's advice, Gandhi traveled around India, and he chose to do so in third-class railroad cars. In South Africa, he had resented being ordered to travel third class, but his views had since changed. Traveling in this way was now part of his desire to identify with ordinary Indians. Everywhere he went, he found a country that was neglected under the British. The vast majority of Indians were desperately poor and uneducated, with little self-respect. Gandhi realized that India needed to do more than simply throw off UK rule. Social reform was also essential, particularly of the Hindu caste system that promoted inequality and that outlawed the Untouchables.

Gandhi came to believe that little would change unless ordinary people joined the struggle for independence. Otherwise, India could simply swap its UK masters for a new elite—the middle-class, Western-educated Indians who made up the Indian National Congress. Gandhi wanted to widen the scope of the organization to include poor farmers and laborers. Only then could true freedom be achieved.

active role in politics. In the meantime, he should travel around India and get to know it again. Gandhi took this advice.

At the end of his travels, Gandhi returned to his naive Gujarat, where he set up another community, called the *Satyagraha Ashram*. The 200-member community ate simple food they grew themselves.[2] At Gandhi's urging, the community admitted a family of Untouchables, although some members left in protest.

First campaigns in India

In 1916, Gandhi made a passionate speech at the opening of the Hindu University of Benares. He expressed his anger not only at the British, but also at wealthy princes and middle-class Indians. The audience contained many wealthy supporters of the university, and some people walked out in protest.

The following year, Gandhi led his first *satyagraha* campaign in India. It was on behalf of poor farmers from Champaran, in northeastern India, who grew indigo (blue plant dye) for dyeing cloth. These peasants were very badly treated by their English landlords, who demanded all the profits from the crop. Gandhi was arrested and thrown in prison again, but he was later released. Eventually, the white plantation-owners reduced the profits they demanded. The success of the campaign was widely reported. Gandhi was becoming well known as a champion of the poor.

Gandhi (seated on dais) addresses a group of boy scouts around 1915. He is wearing just a simple loincloth.

Harsh measures

In 1918, World War I ended. INC leaders hoped that the United Kingdom would now reward India with greater independence, as it had promised—but, instead, UK rule became harsher. In 1919, the United Kingdom introduced a series of laws aimed at stopping any rebellion in India. Called the Rowlatt Acts, these laws allowed the British to imprison anyone suspected of plotting rebellion, without giving the person a proper trial.

In response, Gandhi came up with a new form of protest: the *hartal*, or peaceful strike. Indians everywhere were to protest by withdrawing their labor. Schools, stores, and factories would close. The whole country would come to a halt as protesters marched and prayed. As always, the protest would be nonviolent, reflecting the idea of ahimsa.

Massacre at Amritsar

The day of action did not go as planned, because the strike was not entirely peaceful. In a few places, when the British responded with force, Indians rioted in response. Gandhi called off the strike.

But a British officer named General Dyer decided to "teach the Indians a lesson."[3] On April 13, 1919, he ordered his troops to fire on peaceful demonstrators in an enclosed square in the northwestern city of Amritsar. The soldiers fired 1,650 bullets, until their ammunition ran out, killing 379 and wounding 1,137 men, women, and children.[4] The whole nation was horrified and outraged.

Spinning as resistance

Gandhi spent about an hour every day spinning thread on a hand-driven spinning wheel. This seemed a surprising occupation for a lawyer, but it was in fact part of the drive for India to become self-sufficient.

Under the Raj, India traditionally exported all its raw cotton to the United Kingdom, where it was spun and woven into clothing. Garments were then imported back to India at high prices. If Indians spun their own cotton, there would be less for export. The thread was woven into coarse cloth called *khadi*, which Gandhi encouraged everyone to wear. He himself had given up Western-style clothing and mostly wore just a simple *dhoti*, or loincloth, like a poor farmer. During the **noncooperation** campaign, clothes made in the United Kingdom were burned on bonfires all over India. The *charkha*, or spinning wheel, became a symbol of the INC.

Gandhi said: "When a government takes up arms against its unarmed subjects then it has forfeited [given up] the right to govern."[5]

Gandhi now called for a new stage of resistance that he called noncooperation. He urged Indians everywhere, including soldiers, lawyers, and factory workers, to stop working for the British. He also encouraged Indians to **boycott** goods made in Britain, such as cloth (see the box). In 1915, the great Indian poet and writer Rabrindranath Tagore had called Gandhi "Mahatma," meaning "Great Soul." Increasing numbers of people now began to use that name.

Party reform

In 1920, Gandhi took a leading role in the Indian National Congress. He revised the party constitution, drastically reducing the membership fee so that anyone could join. The whole party took up Gandhi's idea that the INC should work for home rule, although some Muslim members would have preferred to work for reform under the British. The INC also pledged to end the bad treatment of the Untouchables.

Gandhi encouraged all Indians to spin cloth as a means of helping India to be self-sufficient.

Noncooperation takes hold

Throughout 1920 and 1921, the noncooperation campaign gathered momentum, causing disruption throughout British India. The British responded harshly. Many protesters were killed or badly beaten. By 1921, 20,000 demonstrators had been jailed, including Gandhi, and the prisons were full.

What do you think?:

Calling off noncooperation

Was Gandhi right to call off noncooperation after the violence in Chauri Chaura? Huge numbers of people were now taking part in the resistance, so a few violent incidents were probably unavoidable. Some INC leaders felt it was a great shame to stop the campaign in full swing, when it was becoming really effective. Had it continued, the British might have been forced to give in to INC demands.

But Gandhi himself believed it was essential to achieve the just goal of independence by nonviolent means. He wrote: "It is indeed a million times better to appear untrue before the world than to be untrue to ourselves."[6] In other words, Gandhi believed the means were as important as the end, or goal. What do you think? Was the principle of nonviolence too important to sacrifice, even in the cause of achieving independence?

Still, the British would not budge. The Indian National Congress now voted to move to outright **civil disobedience** in a district called Bardoli, near Bombay. This campaign would include nonpayment of taxes. But before it could happen, violence broke out in the northern town of Chauri Chaura. Indian policemen who had fired on demonstrators were chased to their police station, which was set on fire. Twenty-two policemen died. After hearing this news, Gandhi called off the noncooperation campaign, stopping the resistance movement.

Healing discord

In 1922, Gandhi was sentenced to six years in prison. He was released after just two years, after suffering from appendicitis. Meanwhile, there had been growing distrust and unrest between Hindus and Muslims in parts of India. For centuries, followers of the two faiths had lived together throughout India, but there were always tensions. Muslims dominated the population in northwest and northeast India, but in other areas they were in the minority.

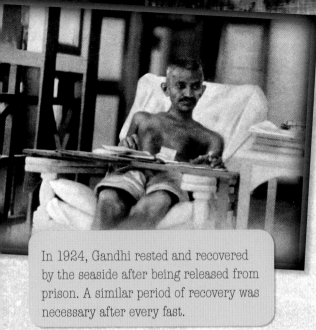

In 1924, Gandhi announced he would begin a fast—and continue until death if needed—in an effort to force Hindu and Muslim communities to resolve their differences. He was now 55 years old. After 21 days, Muslim and Hindu leaders agreed to bury their differences, and Gandhi called off his fast.[7]

In 1924, Gandhi rested and recovered by the seaside after being released from prison. A similar period of recovery was necessary after every fast.

In 1927, the UK government appointed a commission to investigate the matter of Indian independence. But the so-called Simon Commission did not include a single Indian. In response, Gandhi and INC leader Motilal Nehru issued an ultimatum (final demand). Either the United Kingdom should grant India full **dominion** status—self-rule within the British Empire—within a year, or the INC would launch a new disobedience campaign.

Jawaharlal Nehru 1889–1964

Born: Allahabad, India

Role: Leader of the Indian National Congress, 1929 to 1964

Jawaharlal Nehru was the son of lawyer and INC leader Motilal Nehru. He was educated in India and the United Kingdom, where he studied law. He became INC president in 1929. In 1947, Nehru became India's first prime minister, a position he held until his death.

Did you know? Unlike Gandhi, Nehru was not religious. But the two men were very close. Nehru called Gandhi "Bapu," meaning "Father."

Gandhi and Jawaharlal Nehru share a joke during a political meeting. Despite the differences in their ages, the two were very close.

Battle for Independence

In 1929, the viceroy representing the United Kingdom announced that India would be given dominion status at some point in the future. This vague promise was not enough. On January 1, 1930, the new INC president, Jawaharlal Nehru, declared Indian independence. The INC called on all Indians to pledge themselves to nonviolent disobedience—for example, by withholding taxes—until the United Kingdom granted full independence.

Nehru asked Gandhi to lead a new *satyagraha* campaign. Gandhi was unsure what the campaign should focus on. He wanted something that would capture everyone's imagination and demonstrate the injustice of UK rule. Finally, he decided on salt.

The Salt March

Why did Gandhi choose salt? Salt is vital to human health, particularly in hot countries, where the body loses a lot of salt due to sweating. Salt can easily be made from seawater. But in India, the British taxed salt and had made it illegal for Indians to gather and sell salt from their own coasts. This would be a bit like your government deciding to tax the air you breathe.

So, Gandhi decided to march from his ashram in Gujarat to the coast at Dandi to gather salt. The distance was 241 miles.[1] As usual, he informed the authorities of his intentions. The British thought the idea was ridiculous—but they had not taken into account Gandhi's uncanny ability to find an inspiring cause. The Salt March was to be one of his greatest campaigns.

On March 12, Gandhi set off with 78 followers. The march became a

Journalists' cameras clicked in 1930 as Gandhi (seen behind on the left) stooped to gather salt—a simple gesture that symbolized resistance to UK rule.

long procession as thousands joined. Reaching the sea after 24 days, Gandhi bent down and scooped up a pinch of salt. As news of his action spread, people gathered salt all around India's coasts.

Gandhi next planned to march on the British-owned Dharasana Saltworks, north of Bombay. But he had been arrested on May 4. So had 60,000 others who collected salt in defiance of the law. Another INC leader, the female poet Sarojini Naidu, led the march. On May 21, 2,500 unarmed protesters formed orderly rows and advanced on the saltworks, only to be beaten back by the heavy, steel-tipped sticks of policemen. Two protesters died, and 320 were seriously injured.[2]

An Indian policeman mounted on horseback attacks unarmed protesters with his steel-tipped baton during a demonstration at a saltworks.

Eyewitness to the Dharasana protest

U.S. journalist Webb Miller was present at the saltworks protest. His account appeared in over 1,000 newspapers worldwide, convincing many of the injustice of UK rule. He wrote:

"Not one of the marchers even raised an arm to fend off the blows. They went down like ten-pins [bowling pins]. From where I stood I heard the sickening whacks of the clubs on unprotected skulls. The watching crowds groaned and sucked in their breaths in sympathetic pain at every blow… In two or three minutes the ground was quilted with bodies. Great patches of blood widened on their white clothes. The survivors without breaking ranks silently and doggedly marched on until struck down. At times the spectacle of unresisting men being methodically bashed into a bloody pulp sickened me so much I had to turn away."[3]

The United Kingdom begins to back down

After seeing the widespread condemnation of its handling of the salt protest, the United Kingdom realized it had to give in—at least on the issue of salt. In 1931, Gandhi was released from prison and summoned to meet the viceroy, Lord Irwin. Irwin promised to free all protesters and allow Indians to make salt if Gandhi called off the protest. Gandhi agreed.

Gandhi was also invited to go to London to attend a "Round Table Conference" (meaning a conference in which everyone has equal status) about India. A similar conference had been held the previous year, but there were no INC representatives, as almost all INC leaders were then in prison.

Gandhi at the Round Table talks in London in 1931. Conflicting interests among Indian politicians made progress difficult.

Round Table talks

In September 1931, Gandhi attended the conference in London. Sarojini Naidu also represented the Indian National Congress. Other Indian political groups, such as the **Muslim League** and the Untouchables, were also there.

Churchill on Gandhi

UK Conservative Party politician Winston Churchill—who later became the United Kingdom's prime minister—was one of Gandhi's sternest critics. He had expressed disgust at the meeting between Gandhi and Irwin in 1931, saying: "It is alarming and also nauseating to see Mr. Gandhi, a seditious [working against authority] Middle Temple lawyer, now posing as a fakir [type of holy man] of a type well-known in the East, striding half-naked up the steps of the Vice-regal palace…to parley [speak] on equal terms with the representative of the King-Emperor."[4] Even by the UK standards of the time, Churchill's views were extreme. Unfortunately for India, he would become prime minister in 1940.

Gandhi's visit was a great success in terms of publicity. He stayed in London's East End, a poor district. He met celebrities and had tea with the king and queen wearing only his usual shawl and loincloth. He travelled north to meet millworkers. Even though they had been put out of work by his spinning campaign (see page 18), the millworkers supported Gandhi's cause. One worker said: "I am one of the unemployed, but if I was in India I would say the same thing that Mr. Gandhi is saying."[5]

The conference itself was less successful. Representatives of India's minority groups, such as Muslims, Sikhs, Anglo-Indians, and Untouchables, were all concerned about protecting the interests of their own groups, and they demanded **separate electorates**. This meant their members would vote only for seats reserved for them in an Indian parliament—instead of fighting for every seat and losing most to candidates representing the Hindu majority. Gandhi claimed to speak for all Indians, not just Hindus. His cherished aim was a united India, with all religions and castes living in harmony. When the conference ended without agreement, he said it was "the most humiliating day of my life."[6]

Gandhi met with Lancashire millworkers during his visit to Britain in 1931. The millworkers supported his cause.

Gandhi reached home to find there had been a crackdown in his absence. Fearing a fresh wave of protest after the failure of the London talks, the new viceroy had outlawed all rallies, strikes, and political groups. About 35,000 INC members had been jailed. In 1932, Gandhi was arrested without any charges against him, and he joined Nehru in Yeravda Prison, near Pune.

Gandhi's epic fast

In prison, Gandhi heard that the British were planning separate electorates for minority groups such as the Untouchables. Now 63 years old, Gandhi decided to fast "until death" to overturn this decision. After six days, when he was near death, a compromise was reached. The new electorates would be only a temporary measure. Under the so-called Yeravda Pact, caste barriers were also broken down, and Untouchables were allowed to use temples and wells from which they had been banned for many centuries.[7]

Rural reform

In 1933, Gandhi was released from prison. The following year, he resigned from the Indian National Congress, trusting Nehru to steer India toward independence. He probably felt independence was now definitely going to happen–but unity was not, and so he could best serve his country outside party politics.

Gandhi spent most of the next seven years covering huge distances on foot as he toured India's villages. Everywhere he went, he encouraged **hygiene**, education, the rights of women, and, of course, unity among India's peoples. He set up a new ashram at Sevagram in central India, which he and Kasturbai made their home.

Provincial rule

In 1935, Britain took a step toward granting India its independence. The Government of India Act divided India into 11 administrative provinces in which Indians were given control over

Gandhi walking with members of his ashram in the 1930s. During his travels throughout India he identified with poor farmers and their problems.

local matters. However, Britain was still in overall control, with responsibility for finance, foreign policy, and national laws.

Gandhi was unimpressed by the new act. But the Indian National Congress took part in the first provincial elections in 1937 and won control of 9 out of 11 provinces. The Muslim League, now led by Mohammed Ali Jinnah, did not perform well, because most Muslims supported the Indian National Congress. Jinnah now began a campaign to persuade Muslims to switch allegiance to the Muslim League, on the grounds that the league alone represented their interests. The league quickly became more popular.

Meanwhile, in Europe, World War II was approaching, as Adolf Hitler's Germany began a policy of military aggression.

Mohammed Ali Jinnah 1876–1948

Born: Gujarat, India

Role: President of the All-India Muslim League, 1934 to 1947

Mohammed Ali Jinnah's early life bears certain similarities to Gandhi's. Like Gandhi, he was born in Gujarat to a family with a merchant background. He studied law in London and then returned to India and joined the Indian National Congress. But Jinnah resigned from the Indian National Congress in 1920 over Gandhi's noncooperation policy. He believed in working for reform under UK rule. In 1934, he became president of the Muslim League. Not long after, he began campaigning for India to be divided into Hindu and Muslim states.

Did you know? In 1946, the *New York Times* voted Jinnah one of the best-dressed men in the British Empire.[8]

Decision Time

Suddenly, events in Europe began to move rapidly, and the war soon engulfed much of the world. This would result in Gandhi's call for the British to "Quit India."

In 1939, Germany (under Adolf Hitler) invaded Poland, and then the United Kingdom declared war on Germany. Just as it had in 1914, the United Kingdom declared that India was also at war with Germany. This was without any consultation with Indian politicians, exposing how little power India actually had in its current setup of partial home rule.

Gandhi was not active in the Indian National Congress in 1939. His views on the war were somewhat different from other INC leaders. Above all, Gandhi was now a pacifist (person opposed to war). His horror of war outweighed even an intense dislike of the **fascism** guiding Hitler and other leaders in the war. In the

Winston Spencer Churchill 1874–1965

Born: Oxfordshire, England

Role: UK prime minister, 1940 to 1945 and 1951 to 1955

Born into a powerful English family, Winston Churchill graduated from Sandhurst military college and became an officer in a cavalry (horseback) regiment. He served near Afghanistan and also began to work as a reporter. His regiment later fought in Sudan, Africa, and Churchill also reported on the Boer War in South Africa. He entered UK politics in 1900.

When he became prime minister in 1940, Churchill was already known for his opposition to Indian independence. His speeches kept up UK **morale** throughout World War II, but surprisingly, his party lost the general election immediately after the war (see page 40).

past, he had loyally supported the British Empire, organizing the Indian Ambulance Corps in South Africa and even recruiting for the British Army during World War I. But nonviolence was now of the utmost importance to Gandhi. Nehru's view was slightly different. For him, a hatred of fascism and Hitler's Nazis probably outweighed a love of peace.

After considerable debate, the Indian National Congress offered to support the United Kingdom in the war—in return for a promise of greater independence. But the British were in no mood to make a deal, and the new viceroy, Lord Linlithgow, made no such promise. In response, the Indian National Congress refused to cooperate with the United Kingdom. INC ministers in the provinces resigned from their positions, and the UK-led Indian civil service again took on the job of running the subcontinent.[1]

In 1940 and 1941, Germany and its **ally**, Italy, won a series of major victories in Europe, conquering France, the Netherlands, Greece, and much of Scandinavia. The Indian National Congress again offered to support the United Kingdom—in return for immediate independence. But the United Kingdom, now under Prime Minister Winston Churchill, refused outright. After taking office, Churchill had said: "I have not become the King's First Minister in order to preside over the liquidation [giving away] of the British Empire."[2]

The Indian National Congress now looked to Gandhi for advice. Gandhi urged active noncooperation with the United Kingdom. Members of the Congress started to speak out against India's involvement in the war. This went against UK regulations, and about 23,000 activists were arrested.[3]

Even though India's most powerful political party was now urging noncooperation, India was still contributing a great deal to the United Kingdom's war effort, showing that the Congress's influence did not extend to all of India. Indian regiments were fighting in Africa and the Middle East. Indian factories were giving supplies to UK troops. Food supplies sent to the front from India were partly responsible for a famine (serious lack of food) in Bengal, eastern India, in 1943 that killed 3 million people.[4]

Japanese conquests

By 1942, a German victory looked quite likely. In 1940, Japan had entered the war in support of Germany, and in 1941 mounted a surprise attack on the U.S. Navy at a base in Pearl Harbor, Hawaii. This brought the United States into the war on the United Kingdom's side. The war became truly global, with fighting throughout the Pacific.

Over the next few months, one UK colony after another fell to Japan, as its forces took Hong Kong, Singapore, Malaya (now called Malaysia), and finally Burma, on the border with India, in 1942. Soon Japanese bombs were falling on Calcutta and other eastern Indian cities. It looked likely that India would be the next to fall to the Axis powers (Germany, Italy, and Japan).

In the United Kingdom, Prime Minister Churchill was under increasing pressure to grant Indian independence—not only from India itself, but also from members of his own government, which was a wartime coalition (alliance) of all political parties. Many believed that an independent India would still be an ally of the United Kingdom. The United States was also pressing for Indian home rule (see the box). Despite his personal opposition to Indian independence, Churchill felt he had to do something to keep India on his side as a very valuable ally.

The Atlantic Charter

In the mid-1900s, the United States was not in favor of the United Kingdom keeping its empire. Instead, the United States favored the establishment of a **commonwealth**, or alliance, of the United Kingdom and its former colonies after they had been granted independence. In 1941, the United Kingdom and the United States signed the Atlantic Charter, an important policy statement by the two nations that helped define their vision of postwar world politics. In signing it, Churchill acknowledged "the right of all people to choose the form of government under which they live."[5] Churchill later claimed that the charter was about Europe and did not apply to the British Empire, but the Americans and many other nations did not accept this.

The Cripps Proposal

In 1942, Churchill commissioned a prominent politician, Stafford Cripps, to travel to India to present the United Kingdom's new proposal for limited Indian independence after the war. The Cripps mission arrived in March. Cripps set out

Sir Stafford Cripps (left),
Jawaharlal Nehru (right)
and other Indian political
leaders take a break during
negotiations in 1942.

Britain's proposals to Indian politicians, including the Indian National Congress and the Muslim League.

Britain now proposed to make India a self-governing dominion within the British Empire. The idea was for an "Indian Union" made up of 11 provinces, each of which would help to write a new constitution. Each province would be free to either opt into or out of the union. India's independent princely states would also have a say in government–and the princes were known to be influenced by Britain.

Gandhi and Nehru were very disappointed by the Cripps Proposal. The plan did not offer an immediate transfer of power, but rather it put off any changes until the war was over. As a dominion, India would still be under British influence. Equally important, it was likely that provinces with a predominantly Muslim population would opt out of a Hindu-dominated state. So, India would become a patchwork of small provinces, rather than one unified country.

Jinnah's Muslim League was also not in favour of the Cripps Proposal. Since 1940, Jinnah had been calling for British India to be divided into two states–a Hindu-dominated India and a Muslim state called Pakistan. (Pakistan means "Land of the Pure.") However, the concept of Pakistan had a flaw: the two areas where Muslims were in the majority, the northwest and northeast, were separated by a Hindu-dominated area that was hundreds of miles across.

The Indian National Congress responds

Gandhi, Nehru, and the other INC leaders rejected the Cripps Proposal. They urged Cripps to negotiate on the terms proposed for independence, but Cripps had no authority to alter the proposal—it was "take it or leave it." Cripps left India on April 12, blaming Gandhi for the failure of his mission.

The failure of the Cripps mission left Gandhi and the other INC leaders with a dilemma. The breakdown of talks left India still occupied by a foreign power, with increasing numbers of Indians, particularly young activists, bitterly resenting UK rule. At the same time, increasing numbers of Muslims were supporting Jinnah's vision of an independent Pakistan. The Muslim League was becoming much more popular. Last, but certainly not least, the Japanese might invade India at any moment.

Quit India

On April 13, 1942, Gandhi was thinking and praying when a simple two-word slogan came to him: "Quit India." The idea was not that every single British person should leave India immediately. Rather, he was calling for an immediate and full transfer of power to Indian politicians. If the United Kingdom refused, it would face a comprehensive nonviolent rebellion against its rule. The aim was to make India ungovernable for the British.

Gandhi became convinced that only immediate independence would give India the boost in morale it needed to stop Japanese invasion. Without the boost of

What do you think?:

Gandhi's dilemma

What should the Indian National Congress's next move have been? The party looked to Gandhi for advice, even though he had been less involved in politics. For decades now, he had been calling for full independence from the United Kingdom. Some of Gandhi's colleagues argued that if the United Kingdom should withdraw right then, it would leave India at risk of Japanese attack. On the other hand, a UK-dominated India might provoke Japanese attack, whereas a free India would not. Think through the options. What do you think the party's next move should have been? Remember Gandhi's love of nonviolence. What do you think he would advise?

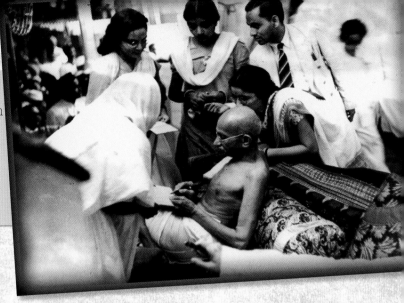

Gandhi at the All-India Congress. He can be seen here giving signatures. He charged a small fee for each signature, to raise money to aid the Untouchables.

independence, a demoralized India was likely to be conquered by Japan, as the other British colonies had been. (As always, Gandhi believed that India should resist any attacks purely through non-violent means.) Nehru and the other INC leaders approved Gandhi's resolution and agreed to propose the campaign at a major conference in August.

On August 7 and 8, 1942, at the All-India Congress Committee meeting in the Gowalia Tank grounds in Bombay, Nehru put forward Gandhi's resolution. He called upon Britain to withdraw from India immediately or face a campaign of a nationwide *satyagraha*, led by Gandhi. In front of a crowd of thousands, Nehru urged "for the vindication of India's inalienable [incapable of being given up] right to freedom and independence, the starting of a mass struggle on non-violent lines on the widest possible scale."[6] The resolution was passed unanimously (by everyone).

Decisive words: Do or die

At the meeting at Gowalia Tank, Gandhi urged Indians to be steadfast in their nonviolent disobedience to the British. He warned that the viceroy might try to strike a bargain, arguing:

"But I will say 'Nothing less than freedom.'… Here is a mantra, a short one, that I give you. You may imprint it on your heart and let every breath of yours give an expression to it. The mantra is 'do or die.' We shall either free India or die in the attempt; we shall not live to see the perpetuation of our slavery."[7]

The Impact of Quit India

The meeting of the Indian National Congress broke up in the early hours of August 9, allowing Gandhi and his supporters only a few hours of sleep before being rudely awakened by a pounding on the door (see pages 4 and 5). After launching the Quit India campaign, Gandhi had expected to have three weeks to negotiate with the viceroy before unleashing the nonviolent *satyagraha*.[1] This assumption was based on his experience of previous campaigns, but it proved incorrect when dealing with the United Kingdom during a time of war.

The British responded with an immediate crackdown. The viceroy himself had given secret orders for Gandhi and other INC leaders to be arrested in raids at dawn across Bombay. This is what led to Gandhi and his close followers being roused from their beds in Birla House, bundled into police cars, and whisked through the streets to the main railroad station, where a special train transported them to Yeravda Prison near Poona (Puna), in northwest India. Gandhi's wife, Kasturbai, joined them the following day, having been arrested on her way to address a meeting. Nehru and the other INC leaders were jailed elsewhere. Instead of facing the viceroy, Gandhi faced the walls of a prison cell.

Violence and British crackdown

News of Gandhi's call for action and arrest spread like wildfire across India. It triggered widespread action, including strikes and demonstrations. But without Gandhi or other INC leaders to guide the uprising, many demonstrations turned violent. Symbols of UK rule such as government offices and police stations were burned down. Railroads were torn up, and British officials

Decisive words: International news

A writer working for the U.S. magazine *Time* reflected on the dramatic events of August 9, saying:

"In a crisis caused by Mohandas Karamchand Gandhi's threat of open revolt, the British struck first. The slamming of jail doors on the leaders of the Indian National Congress party was their answer to Gandhi's demand for immediate Indian independence."[2]

were attacked and killed. The violence was the worst in the north, including in the capital, Delhi. In response, the British banned all public meetings, demonstrations, and marches and outlawed the Indian National Congress itself. On a prearranged signal, police moved to arrest not only INC leaders, but also activists throughout India.

On August 31, 1942, Viceroy Linlithgow reported to Churchill: "I am engaged here in meeting by far the most serious rebellion since that of 1857, the gravity [seriousness] and extent of which we have so far concealed from the world."[3] Linlithgow was referring to the 1857 Mutiny in India (see page 6). But there was one big difference between the current situation and the 1857 Mutiny: this time, the Indian Army remained loyal to the British, as did the Indian police.

In 1942, Indian police used smoke bombs to disperse crowds that gathered to protest Gandhi's arrest. Here, the dense smoke has forced people to lie on the ground.

Britain smashed the rebellion with all forces under its command. The police and army opened fire on stone-throwing demonstrators and even machine-gunned some crowds from the air. The most rebellious regions were bombed. As it was at war, Britain had neither the time nor the energy to fine-tune its response in order to avoid bad publicity—and, in any case, the government had special wartime powers that gave it more control over what was reported. About 60,000 people were arrested, but still thousands more joined the resistance.

Churchill's response

In Britain, Churchill accused Gandhi of causing the violence. He announced: "The Congress Party has now abandoned its policy of non-violence...and has come into the open as a revolutionary movement."[4] Gandhi protested against this "slaughter of the truth."[5] He maintained that it was the British crackdown that was causing the violence. Gandhi began a new fast in protest. But the viceroy held firm this time, dismissing the fast as "a form of political blackmail."[6] Gandhi fasted for three weeks before calling off his protest, and he nearly died in the process.

Death of Gandhi's secretary

Gandhi's secretary, Mahadev Desai, was imprisoned with him on August 9. But after less than a week in prison, Desai suddenly collapsed and died. He had been with Gandhi for 25 years. Desai was much more than a secretary. He was Gandhi's adopted son and one of his closest aids, with whom the Mahatma discussed all of his ideas. Desai's death was a bitter blow for Gandhi.

Did Quit India succeed?

On August 8, Gandhi and the Indian National Congress had called for all Indians to join in a nationwide disobedience campaign, with the aim of making India ungovernable. Tens of thousands had answered the call, from factory workers and farmers to middle-class professionals such as lawyers and doctors. In some districts, the rebels had managed to overthrow the regional government and set up their own administration. However, Gandhi's call for action did not receive the overwhelming support for which he and other leaders had hoped.

Britain retained the support of the state and imperial police, the Indian Army, and the country's civil service. The princely states also remained loyal. So did many Indian businessmen, including industrialists and traders, who were prospering in wartime. In all of these groups, most individuals benefited from the British administration or were bound by ties of loyalty and discipline. In addition, it is likely that a great many people feared that a Japanese invasion would follow swiftly after a British withdrawal from India.

The Indian National Congress also did not succeed in rallying other political parties to its cause. The Communist Party of India supported Britain and the war, because it wished to support Britain's ally, the Soviet Union. The Muslim League under Jinnah also refused to support the Indian National Congress, and many small parties followed suit. All of these groups had their own ideas about exactly when and how Indian independence should be achieved and did not share the Congress's vision. The Indian National Congress also did not gain international support–the United States, known to be in favour of independence, quietly fell in line behind Britain after pressure from Churchill.

In all, Gandhi's call for mass disobedience failed to inspire the level of support it needed to make India truly ungovernable. Britain succeeded in quieting the revolt within months. Nonetheless, the campaign did lead to change. The level of resistance forced the British government to realize that it could not hold on to India in the long term. It would have no choice but withdrawal after the war.

These women were among the protesters during the Quit India campaign.

Report on the riots

At the end of 1942, most of the Quit India riots had been suppressed. The British took stock of the destruction caused by the turmoil. A total of 1,318 government buildings and 208 police stations had been destroyed; 3,400 telephone or telegraph lines had been damaged; and 332 railroad stations had been wrecked.[7] All this destruction had seriously hindered the war effort.

The costs of the British crackdown had been high, too. The British estimated that between 1,000 and 2,000 demonstrators had been killed. The Indian National Congress put the figure much higher– at between 4,000 and 10,000 people.[8]

Death of Kasturbai and Gandhi's release

Early in 1944, Gandhi suffered another personal tragedy. The previous year, his beloved wife, Kasturbai, had developed a lung infection. Gandhi refused to allow the doctor to give her penicillin because he disapproved of Western-style medicine, including injections of antibiotics. On February 22, Kasturbai died in her husband's arms. The couple had

The Indian National Army

If the unrest caused by Quit India was not enough, the British also faced a new enemy within India. In 1942, a former INC activist named Subash Chandra Bose had requested help from Japan and Germany to launch a military uprising against the British. The Japanese allowed him to recruit 40,000 prisoners of war from their detention camps. These Indian soldiers had been captured by the Japanese while defending UK colonies such as Singapore. This army of recruits, called the Indian National Army, launched attacks against UK forces in 1943. But in 1944, the UK-led Indian Army forced them to retreat.[9]

Indian troops loyal to the British Empire played a prominent part in World War II. Here Indian soldiers attack enemy tanks in Egypt in 1940.

been together for 62 years. In the early days, they had had their differences, but for decades now they had been very close.

Not long after, Gandhi himself became sick with the disease malaria and then dysentery. Fearing that a new wave of violence might erupt if Gandhi died in prison, the viceroy decided to release him. He was set free on May 6, 1944, after nearly two years in prison.

Talks with Jinnah

After a short period of rest and recovery, Gandhi again became active in politics. But his goal was not a fresh campaign against the British. Resentment over British rule was now so widespread that independence seemed inevitable. However, Gandhi's hopes of a free, united India were now seriously threatened by the growing strength of the All-India Muslim League.

Since 1942, the Muslim League had been cooperating with the British. But the league's leader, Jinnah, had made it clear that Muslim support was given in exchange for a separate Muslim state being seriously considered after the war was over. Meanwhile, he had continued to persuade Muslim INC supporters to leave the party and join the Muslim League. The Muslim League had become stronger than ever before.

Gandhi and Mohammed Ali Jinnah during talks in 1944. Despite the smiles, the two leaders could not agree on India's future.

In September 1944, Gandhi met Jinnah for three weeks of talks. Gandhi's aim was to reach an agreement that would make the two-state solution unnecessary. However, Jinnah would not compromise. He insisted that the Muslim League now spoke for all Muslims. The talks ended without agreement. The only result was that Jinnah's standing as a national leader was increased by his talks with Gandhi.

End of World War II

By 1944, Britain and its allies, the United States and the Soviet Union, had halted the German and Japanese advance and were winning back lost territory. The tide of the war was turning. In May 1945, Germany surrendered. Japan then surrendered in August. The long, bitter war was over.

In India, Nehru and the other INC activists were freed, and negotiations began again. Both the United States and the Soviet Union now put pressure on Churchill to grant India its independence. But Churchill was still reluctant. At talks in June, the British were content to allow differences between Hindus and Muslims to prevent any progress.

But the nationalist cause now received an unexpected boost. In July 1945, Britain held a general election. Churchill's government was defeated, and a new government, under Clement Attlee, took control.

The new government represented the Labour Party, which was in favour of Indian home rule. The Labour Party had been more open to home rule in the 1930s, and now the Quit India protests had convinced many Labour politicians that trying to hold on to India was a waste of energy and resources. Attlee's government wanted Britain to withdraw from India–as quickly as possible. It announced that elections would be held in India that winter, and that a new National Assembly would draw up a constitution.

Indian election

In the period before the elections, Jinnah campaigned hard to win all Muslim voters. He painted a bleak picture of what life would be like for Muslims under a Hindu-dominated government, which he called a "Hindu Raj." When the election results were announced, it was clear that Jinnah's tactic had been successful. The Muslim League won all 30 of the seats saved for Muslims in the National Assembly. They also won many seats in the provinces, although the Indian National Congress won a clear majority overall.[10] Jinnah could now more fairly claim that the Muslim League spoke for all Muslims.

The Simla Conference

In 1946, Attlee announced that a conference on the future of India would be held in the hill town of Simla. All Indian political parties would be represented, along with a three-man British cabinet mission, led by Stafford Cripps (see pages 30 to 32). However, the talks could not lead to agreement, due to Jinnah's insistence on the division of India–also called **partition**–and the creation of the Muslim state of Pakistan. The talks broke up without agreement, and with no solution in sight.

Jawaharlal Nehru and Mohammed Ali Jinnah pose for the press during talks in 1946.

Views on partition

Gandhi was deeply opposed to Jinnah's vision of a divided India and the formation of Pakistan. Moreover, partition did not make much sense in terms of India's population. Millions of Hindus lived in the area that would become Pakistan, and millions of Muslims lived in what would become India. The proposed state of Pakistan was made up of two regions—the Punjab in the northwest and Bengal in the east. The large distance between the two would make Pakistan very difficult to govern.

The British were also initially opposed to partition. They had hoped the talks would result in the creation of a unified, independent India, which they could do business with. Cripps therefore proposed a compromise: a federation of two mainly independent groups of provinces, one mainly Hindu and the other mainly Muslim, under a central government with weak powers. This solution was acceptable to Nehru and Gandhi, but not to Jinnah, so it was abandoned.

Independence and Partition

In 1946, the British cabinet mission appointed the head of India's new National Assembly. They chose Nehru, as he was the leader of the most popular party. Nehru offered Jinnah a role in government, but he refused to have any part in it. Instead, Jinnah announced a Day of Action on August 16, 1946. He called on all Muslims to demonstrate the strength of their support for an independent state of Pakistan. Unlike Gandhi, Jinnah did not stress the need for non-violence.

On August 16, rioting broke out between Hindus and Muslims on a scale never seen before. The violence was worse in the northern provinces, where Hindu and Muslim populations were roughly equal: Punjab, Bihar, and Bengal. In the city of Calcutta, in Bengal, 5,000 died and 15,000 were injured. Tens of thousands more were killed elsewhere, with **massacres** being committed by both sides.[1]

Gandhi, who had taken a less active role in recent talks, now took the lead in trying to restore peace. At the age of 75, he travelled to Bengal. There, he went on foot from village to village, praying and calling on Muslims and Hindus to resolve their differences. His tactic worked, but even Gandhi could not be in more than one place at a time. Leaving Bengal, he went to Bihar to try to restore peace there.

Lord Louis Mountbatten 1900–1979

Born: Windsor, Berkshire, England

Role: Last viceroy/governor-general of India, 1947 to 1948

A member of the UK royal family, Lord Louis Mountbatten joined the Royal Navy at the age of 16. As the last viceroy of India, he finally urged the division of India into two states as the only alternative to civil war. After Indian independence, he returned to the navy where he rose to become first sea lord, the highest position in the Royal Navy. He retired in 1965.

Did you know? Mountbatten said of Jinnah: "If it could be said that any single man held the future of India in the palm of his hand in 1947, that man was Mohammed Ali Jinnah."[2]

Lord Louis Mountbatten and his wife meet with Gandhi in New Dehli. Mountbatten, the last British viceroy, had the difficult task of overseeing India in the last months before independence.

But some Hindu **extremists** refused to be **reconciled** and claimed that Gandhi was pro-Muslim. Violence continued to flare.

Notice to quit

By February 1947, Attlee's government had decided it would be best to leave as soon as possible, even with no clear picture of India's future. Britain announced it would withdraw from India by June 1948 at the latest. A new viceroy, Lord Louis Mountbatten, would oversee the transfer of power to "responsible hands." However, no one knew exactly who or what would take control.

Mountbatten arrived in March. He immediately held talks with Gandhi, Nehru, and Jinnah to try to reach agreement. Jinnah threatened that **civil war** would follow if India was not partitioned. In desperation, Gandhi proposed that Jinnah become prime minister of a new, united India, but neither Nehru nor Jinnah could agree to this. Meanwhile, violence between Hindus and Muslims was still increasing.

Mountbatten decided to move the date for independence forward to the summer of 1947, to avoid chaos and civil war. It had become quite clear that Jinnah would never agree to a unified India. The only other option was to persuade INC leaders to agree to partition. Finally, Nehru agreed, but not Gandhi. It was the end of Gandhi's dream of a united India.

Preparing for independence

In July 1947, the British government passed the Indian Independence Act. What had been British India would become two independent states: a Hindu-dominated India and a Muslim-dominated Pakistan (made of two parts, West Pakistan and East Pakistan). The princely states would merge with India or Pakistan.

This map shows the partition of the Indian subcontinent into India and Pakistan in 1947, and the movements of refugees following partition.

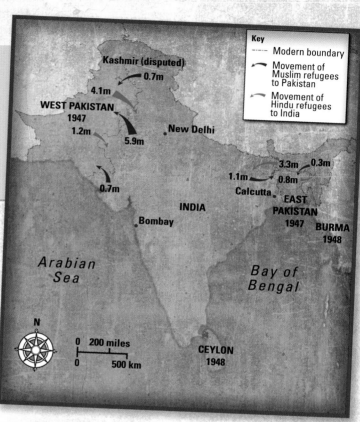

Key
- - - - Modern boundary
Movement of Muslim refugees to Pakistan
Movement of Hindu refugees to India

Kashmir (disputed)
0.7m
4.1m
WEST PAKISTAN
1947
1.2m
5.9m
New Delhi
3.3m   0.3m
1.1m   0.8m
Calcutta   EAST
0.7m   PAKISTAN
INDIA   1947   BURMA
Bombay   1948
Arabian Sea
Bay of Bengal
N
0   200 miles
0   500 km
CEYLON
1948

A boundary commission worked against the clock to decide the borders of the new states. The provinces of Punjab and Bengal, with roughly equal numbers of Hindus and Muslims, were both divided. As soon as the boundaries were known, huge numbers of people began to emigrate (leave their countries). Millions of Hindus and Sikhs started moving from what would be Pakistan into India, and millions of Muslims moved in the opposite direction, to Pakistan. Rioting and bloodshed began as an incredible 12 million people left their homes and fled, taking only the possessions they could carry.

Meanwhile, the British made hasty preparations to leave. A century of direct rule and 350 years of UK influence were finally ending. The nationalist movement, which had begun in the late 1800s, would finally achieve its goal. But the human cost would be very high.

Triumph and tragedy

On August 15, India became a self-governing state. The independent state of Pakistan had come into being the previous day. Millions celebrated, but not Gandhi. Still mourning the loss of unity, he called the day a "spiritual tragedy."[3] He spent the day in Calcutta, helping victims of violence—and trying to calm the turmoil that was now raging.

Arguments had broken out among the long lines of **refugees** moving across borders. Blows were exchanged, then knife wounds and gunfire. Panic and chaos took over, with a huge loss of life. Mobs formed and soon lost all restraint and started to riot, driven by thirst for revenge. Experts believe around a million people died in the violence, including thousands of Sikhs from the Punjab.

Nehru called for calm, but only Gandhi, still in Calcutta, could bring peace. He responded by putting his own life on the line. On September 1, he announced that he would fast until Hindus and Muslims came to their senses and were reconciled. After three days, the tactic worked on a local level in Calcutta. Hindus and Muslims filed past his bedside, pledging peace and laying down their weapons. Gandhi ended his fast. But elsewhere chaos still reigned.

Decisive words: Nehru's Independence Day speech

On August 14, Nehru, India's new prime minister, proclaimed Indian independence, saying:

"Long years ago we made a tryst with destiny, and now the time comes when we shall redeem our pledge, not wholly or in full measure, but very substantially. At the stroke of the midnight hour, when the world sleeps, India will awake to life and freedom."[4]

Decisive words: Gandhi's reaction

In reaction to the violence between refugees, Gandhi wrote in his diary:

"Anger breeds revenge and the spirit of revenge is today responsible for all the horrible happenings here and elsewhere. I implore you all to stop your insane actions at once… Remember that unless we stop this madness the name of India will be mud in the eyes of the world."[5]

Restoring peace

Having brought peace to Calcutta, Gandhi traveled west, to New Delhi. The capital was torn by violence and had received huge numbers of refugees from the Punjab region. On January 13, 1948, Gandhi began a new fast to reconcile people from different faiths. Again, the tactic worked, and Hindu, Muslim, and Sikh leaders agreed to end their differences. Violence also died down elsewhere.

However, some Hindus were angry at Gandhi, because they felt he favored Muslims. On January 20, a Hindu extremist was behind a failed bomb attempt to assassinate (kill) Gandhi. Gandhi commented: "If I should fall victim to an assassin's bullet, there must be no anger within me. God must be in my heart and on my lips."[6]

Death of Gandhi

Just 10 days later, on January 30, a Hindu extremist named Nathuram Godse surprised Gandhi on his way to an evening prayer meeting. Godse produced a revolver and fired several shots at point-blank range. The 78-year-old Gandhi collapsed, gasping. Some say that he spoke the Hindi word *Rama*, meaning "God." He died almost instantly.

Nehru rushed to the scene and wept for the loss of his close friend and counselor. However, he still had the presence of mind to announce on All-India Radio that Gandhi's assassin was a Hindu. This probably prevented a new wave of violence from breaking out.

Decisive words: Nehru's tribute

On January 30, Nehru announced Gandhi's death with a moving speech:

"Friends and comrades, the light has gone out of our lives, and there is darkness everywhere. Our beloved leader…is no more. The light has gone out, I said, and yet I was wrong. For the light that shone in this country was no ordinary light… For that light represented something more than the immediate past, it represented the living, the eternal truths, reminding us of the right path, drawing us from error, taking this ancient country to freedom."[7]

The next day, an enormous crowd of 2 million people attended Gandhi's funeral and cremation (turning a body into ashes by burning). Later, his ashes were scattered on the sacred Jumna River. Millions of Indians considered him a saint, but Gandhi preferred to define himself as a "seeker after truth." Tributes came

not just from India, but from all over the world. The scientist Albert Einstein said: "Generations to come will scarce believe that such a one as this walked the earth in flesh and blood."[8]

Achievements

Gandhi is often called the "father of India." He played a key role in the Indian independence movement. With his alert mind, he invented a new form of protest: *satyagraha*, or non-violent resistance. Aimed at nothing less than converting his opponents to his way of thinking, it inspired millions to join his cause. *Satyagraha* caught the public imagination and attracted huge publicity. It also exposed the way in which British colonial rule exploited the people of India.

In the decades that followed, Gandhi's tactic of non-violence would be taken up by many campaigners, including the US civil rights activist Martin Luther King Jr., and the Burmese pro-**democracy** leader Aung San Suu Kyi.

By carefully choosing his campaigns, Gandhi transformed Indian politics. He changed the Indian National Congress from a small, elite party of middle-class professionals to a mass movement. But Gandhi fought for much more than independence. He also campaigned for social reform. He broke down barriers within the Hindu caste system to improve the status of the Untouchables. He championed the poor and campaigned tirelessly for hygiene, education, and women's rights. Above all, Gandhi worked for unity among the different faiths and peoples of India, a cause for which he finally gave his life.

After independence

In 1950, India adopted its new constitution, becoming an independent republic within the British Commonwealth. As India's prime minister, Nehru steered the new country along the course he had set with Gandhi. He worked to reduce poverty, improve education and women's rights, and break down prejudice against the Untouchables. He also modernized farming and, in particular, industry.

Nehru remained prime minister until his death in 1964. After two years, his daughter, Indira Gandhi (no relation to the Mahatma), succeeded him as prime minister, serving from 1966 to 1977 and again from 1980 to 1984. In turn, Indira Gandhi was succeeded by her son Rajiv (prime minister from 1984 to 1989). In this way, Nehru's descendants have remained important in Indian politics. Mohammed Ali Jinnah became Pakistan's first governor-general in 1947, but he died of cancer in September 1948.

India and Pakistan

Since 1947, relations between India and Pakistan have continued to be troubled. Following the choices made at independence, the two countries have continued to pursue different paths. India is a **secular** (nonreligious) state with a Hindu majority, whereas Pakistan is an Islamic republic with an overwhelmingly Muslim population.

The two countries established diplomatic links soon after partition, meaning they communicated regularly, but conflicts have continued, notably over the northern state of Kashmir. India and Pakistan have fought several wars. In 1971, civil war

Conflict within India

At independence, Nehru's Indian National Congress took control of a nation made up of roughly 275 million Hindus and 50 million Muslims. Other major religious groups included 7 million Christians, 6 million Sikhs, and 100,000 Parsis (followers of the Zoroastrian religion).[9] In addition to many religions, there were, and are, great differences among India's people in terms of culture and language—there are 15 official languages and over 800 dialects.[10] From time to time, conflict has flared between Hindus, Muslims, Sikhs, and other groups in India, but never on a scale remotely approaching that of 1947. India has remained a democracy, with internal problems largely resolved by the democratic process. In contrast, Pakistan has been mainly ruled by generals since 1948.

Soldiers from East Pakistan train during the 1971 conflict between East and West Pakistan. The eventual defeat of West Pakistan led to the creation of Bangladesh.

broke out between West and East Pakistan. India supported East Pakistan and defeated West Pakistan. East Pakistan broke away to become the independent state of Bangladesh.

Modern India

In the early 1990s, India modernized its industries and introduced economic reforms to bring it in line with Western-style economies. Its industries grew very rapidly. It is now one of the world's leading economies and, as a result, it is an important world power. Gandhi would probably not have approved of what he would have seen as the triumph of material values (values related to money and objects) over spirituality. Not long before he died, he spoke of the "vain imitation of the tinsel of the West."[11] However, he would have approved of his country's ability to be self-sufficient and hold its place in the world.

What if...?

Gandhi's Quit India campaign had lasting consequences for India–but the impact was not what Gandhi had intended. In causing the imprisonment of INC leaders until the end of the war, the campaign unintentionally strengthened the Muslim League and probably made partition inevitable.

It is interesting to think about what might have happened if events had not turned out the way they did. What if Quit India had succeeded in making the British leave immediately? What if the British response had been different? Could the Indian subcontinent have become a single, unified state?

What if Britain had left India immediately?

Even if Quit India had been peaceful, the British would probably still have cracked down forcibly, since it was a time of war. However, it is possible that the British might have been forced to transfer power and leave India before the end of the war. This would have left India open to invasion by Japan.

Gandhi's answer to this threat was non-violent protest. In 1938, he wrote: "Refuse to obey Hitler's will and perish unarmed in the attempt. In so doing, though I lose the body, I save my soul."[1] It is possible that Japan would have conquered India. This might have prolonged the war, but the likely outcome would still have been the defeat of the Axis powers.

Could India have been a unified state?

As it turned out, the British imprisoned INC leaders until the end of the war. The power vacuum allowed Jinnah to strengthen his position, paving the way for partition. So, might British India have become a single, unified state without Quit India? Perhaps.

Hindus, Muslims, Sikhs, and other faiths had lived together in villages throughout India for centuries. However, there had always been certain tensions between religious groups–tensions that the British had been quick to exploit, under the old policy of "divide and rule." It is true that within the Indian National Congress, Hindus, Muslims, Sikhs, and other faiths worked together for decades against a common enemy, Britain. However, after the British left, the party–and the country in general–might not have remained so united.

Jinnah is often blamed for stirring up discord between Hindus and Muslims. But India had never been one unified country. For example, there were many princely states. History has shown that conflict has continued between the secular state of India (majority Hindu) and Pakistan (majority Muslim). However, within India itself, religious tensions have mostly been contained. India remains the world's largest democracy, which is a great tribute to both Nehru and Gandhi. Before partition, British India held roughly 300 million Hindus, 100 million Muslims, and 6 million Sikhs.[2] If the subcontinent had become one unified state, the tensions between its many peoples might have been greater.

What do you think?:

Could it have been peaceful?

On August 8, 1942, when he launched Quit India, Gandhi calculated that he had three weeks to negotiate with the viceroy. However, he and all the other INC leaders were arrested immediately. With the leaders absent, the campaign became violent, resulting in a brutal crackdown by the British. Had Gandhi and the other leaders remained free, the campaign might have remained largely peaceful. Think about the success of Gandhi's previous efforts to maintain nonviolence. Could Quit India have been peaceful?

An Indian protester adopts Gandhi's tactic of *satyagraha*. He lies down in front of an ox cart to protest against the forced import of British cloth to India.

Gandhi's Legacy

Some experts think that Gandhi's decision to launch Quit India showed bad judgment—the last desperate attempt of an old man to achieve his goal, no matter the consequences. One commentator has said it "led to disaster."[1] Mohammed Ali Jinnah called it "the Mahatma's Himalayan blunder"—meaning a mistake of huge proportions.[2]

Mahatma Gandhi visits Muslim refugees who have been forced to flee their homes by the partition of India in 1947.

Did Quit India succeed in achieving its aim? That depends on what you define as Gandhi's aim. If the aim was simply to make the United Kingdom leave as soon as possible, the widespread violence and unrest probably did convince the British that it was no longer possible to hold on to India. It probably made the British leave sooner rather than later. However, it is likely that the British would have granted independence not long after the war without Quit India, thanks in part to outside pressure—for example, from the United States and Soviet Union, and also according to the new Labour government's own opinions.

Gandhi's wider aim was to achieve a united India following independence. The Quit India campaign clearly failed to achieve this. Indeed, it resulted in the imprisonment of INC leaders, which allowed the Muslim League to gather strength and press for partition. In this way, it can be said that the impact of Quit India was the opposite of what Gandhi had hoped.

Gandhi's most important decision?

Was Quit India the most important decision of Gandhi's career? It was certainly one of the most far reaching, with an impact that is still felt today. But as we have seen, it was a failure in terms of Gandhi's wider aim. The noncooperation campaigns of the 1920s and the Salt March of 1930 were far more successful in achieving their aims. These campaigns undermined UK rule in India and attracted widespread support for the nationalist cause. On a personal level, Gandhi's fasts—for example, in 1924, 1932, and 1942—were also very successful in achieving their aims, including the incredibly difficult goal of reconciling Hindus, Muslims, and other faiths.

Gandhi's legacy as a leader

More than any other person, Gandhi helped to achieve Indian independence. Without him, there is little doubt that the British would have clung on to India for longer. However, Gandhi's **legacy** goes far beyond a single cause, even Indian independence. Almost single-handedly, he managed to transform the Indian National Congress from a small, elite party into a mass movement. In this way, he paved the way for India to become truly democratic. Gandhi also campaigned for social reform, including better living standards for the poor and the removal of caste barriers surrounding the Untouchables.

Gandhi's political legacy goes beyond India. His greatest gift was probably the invention of *satyagraha*, or non-violent protest. This has since been taken up by many campaign groups around the world, including the civil rights movement in the United States and the anti-apartheid movement in South Africa (where laws divided the races). Gandhi's influence can still be felt whenever people campaign peacefully for a cause they believe in, using non-violence even in the face of violence.

Decisive words: Martin Luther King Jr., on Gandhi

U.S. civil rights leader Martin Luther King Jr., paid tribute to Gandhi, saying:

"Gandhi was inevitable. If humanity is to progress Gandhi is inescapable. He lived, thought, and acted, inspired by the vision of humanity evolving towards a world of peace and harmony. We may ignore him at our own risk."[3]

Timeline

1757

The British East India Company conquers Bengal. This is the start of the British Empire in India.

1858

The UK government takes over control of India from the East India Company following the Indian Mutiny of 1857

1869

Mohandas Karamchand Gandhi is born at Porbandar, in Gujarat province (northwest India), the son of Karamchand and Putlibai Gandhi

1883

Gandhi marries a girl named Kasturbai

1885

The Indian National Congress (INC) is formed Gandhi's father dies

1888

Gandhi travels to England to study law

1928

Gandhi organizes a tax strike in Bardoli, Gujarat province, to protest against the noninclusion of Indians in a UK investigation into Indian independence

1924

Gandhi fasts to encourage Hindus and Muslims to reconcile

1922

Gandhi calls off the noncooperation campaign after violence erupts in Chauri Chaura Gandhi is arrested and sentenced to six years in prison, but he is released after two years

1920

Gandhi organizes a noncooperation campaign to boycott UK goods

1919

Gandhi organizes protests against the Rowlatt Acts The Amritsar Massacre takes place in Amritsar, in Punjab province

1930

The Indian National Congress proclaims Indian independence Gandhi leads the Salt March to protest against a UK act that forbids Indians to make salt

1931

Gandhi represents the Indian National Congress at "Round Table" talks in London, but he is arrested after he returns to India

1932

Gandhi fasts to protest against a UK proposal to have a separate electorate for the Untouchables

1933–1940

Mostly inactive within the Indian National Congress, Gandhi tours India, campaigning against poverty and trying to improve education, hygiene, and women's rights

1947

August 15
British India is partitioned into two states—India and Pakistan—both of which gain independence Widespread violence breaks out between Hindus, Muslims, and Sikhs over the issue of partition Gandhi fasts to achieve reconciliation between Muslims and Hindus in Bengal

The British, under Viceroy Lord Mountbatten, prepare to leave India

1946

August 16
The Muslim League Day of Action results in widespread violence between Muslims and Hindus

1946

May
The Simla Conference takes place. Jinnah continues to press for India to be divided and for the creation of Pakistan.

1948

January
Gandhi fasts to achieve reconciliation between Muslims and Hindus in New Delhi He is shot by a Hindu extremist and dies at the age of 78

1949

Jinnah, now the governor-general of Pakistan, dies of cancer

1950

India adopts a new constitution

1964

Nehru, who has served as India's prime minister since 1947, dies

1966–1977

Nehru's daughter Indira Gandhi serves as India's prime minister

1891
Gandhi obtains a law degree and returns to India

1893
Gandhi travels to South Africa to take up a position with an Indian law firm in the Transvaal

He returns briefly to India and is beaten up by a mob after his return to South Africa

1894
Gandhi works on behalf of Indians in Natal, in South Africa, setting up the Natal Indian Congress

1899
Gandhi organizes the Indian Ambulance Corps to care for injured UK soldiers during the Boer War in South Africa

1904
Gandhi sets up his first community, the Phoenix Settlement, in South Africa

He founds the journal *Indian Opinion*, to provide a voice for South Africa's Indian community

1916
Gandhi makes a speech at Hindu University at Benares

1915
Gandhi returns to India and is welcomed by the Indian National Congress

He travels around India to get to know the country again

He founds the *Satyagraha* Ashram in Gujarat, which includes a family of Untouchables

1914-1918
World War I is fought. The United Kingdom involves India in the war.

1906
Gandhi organizes his first *satyagraha* campaign to protest against a new law that requires Indians in the Transvaal to register and carry an identity card

In India, the Muslim League is formed

1935
The Government of India Act divides India into 11 provinces, which are given self-rule

1939
World War II begins. As in 1914, the United Kingdom involves India in the war.

Gandhi becomes active in politics again

1940
Mohammed Ali Jinnah argues for India to be partitioned, or divided, and for the creation of the Muslim state of Pakistan

1942
March

The Cripps mission, a UK delegation that proposes partial independence, ends in failure

1942
August

Gandhi launches the Quit India campaign

He and other INC leaders are arrested and jailed

Gandhi's secretary, Mahadev Desai, dies in prison

1946
March

The UK cabinet mission arrives in India

Tensions increase between Hindus and Muslims over the prospect of sharing power within an independent India

1945
World War II ends

Nehru and other INC leaders are released

The Labour Party takes power in the United Kingdom. The new UK government resolves to grant India independence as soon as possible.

1944
Gandhi's wife, Kasturbai, dies in prison

Gandhi is released and holds talks with Jinnah, aimed at resolving differences between Jinnah's Muslim League and the Indian National Congress, but the talks fail

1971
Civil war erupts in Pakistan

India defeats West Pakistan, and East Pakistan becomes Bangladesh

1980-1984
Indira Gandhi has her second term as India's prime minister, but in 1984 she is assassinated

1984-1991
Nehru's grandson Ravij Gandhi serves as India's prime minister, but he is assassinated in 1991

1999
Unrest spreads through Kashmir

2001
Tension between India and Pakistan nearly leads to nuclear war, but war is avoided thanks to diplomacy (meeting and discussing the issues)

Notes on Sources

An Arrest in Bombay
(pages 4–5)

1. Finding Dulcinea, "On This Day: Gandhi's Arrest Sparks 'Quit India' Movement," August 9, 2011, http://www.findingdulcinea.com/news/on-this-day/July-August-08/On-this-Day--Gandhi-s-Arrest-Launches-the-Quit-India-Movement.html.

2. *World Book Encyclopedia*, "World War II," http://worldbookonline.com/student/article?id=ar610460&st=world+war+ii.

India Under the Raj
(pages 6–11)

1. *World Book Encyclopedia*, "India," http://worldbookonline.com/student/article?id=ar274440&st=india.

2. Christine Hatt, *Mahatma Gandhi* (Judge for Yourself) (London: Evans Brothers, 2009), 20–21.

3. David Downing, *Mohandas Gandhi* (Leading Lives) (Oxford, Eng.: Heinemann Library, 2002), 10.

4. Catherine Clément and Ruth Sharman, *Gandhi: Father of a Nation* (London: Thames and Hudson, 1996), 17.

5. *World Book Encyclopedia*, "India."

6. Clément and Sharman, *Gandhi: Father of a Nation*, 28.

7. David Cumming, *India* (London: Wayland, 1995), 32.

Birth of a Leader
(pages 12–15)

1. Downing, *Mohandas Gandhi*, 16.

2. Sara Robbins, ed., Law: A *Treasury of Art and Literature* (New York: Beaux Arts Editions, 1990), 87–88, http://bargad.org/2010/12/25/gandhi-sedition/.

3. Downing, *Mohandas Gandhi*, 20.

4. Pankaj Mishra, "Ex-Father of the Nation," *New York Times*, April 15, 2001, http://www.nytimes.com/2001/04/15/books/ex-father-of-the-nation.html?pagewanted=all&src=pm.

5. Downing, *Mohandas Gandhi*, 26..

Noncooperation
(pages 16–21)

1. Clément and Sharman, *Gandhi: Father of a Nation*, 52.

2. Hatt, *Mahatma Gandhi*, 22.

3. Clément and Sharman, *Gandhi: Father of a Nation*, 60.

4. Lawrence James, *Raj: The Making and Unmaking of British India* (London: Little Brown, 1997), 473.

5. Oracle ThinkQuest Education Foundation, "Division Among the Indians," http://library.thinkquest.org/17282/history/divisionamongindians.html.

6. Clément and Sharman, *Gandhi: Father of a Nation*, 65.

7. Ibid., 66.

Battle for Independence
(pages 22–27)

1. The Web Chronology Project, "The Gandhi Salt March 1930," http://thenagain.info/webchron/India/SaltMarch.html.

2. Clément and Sharman, *Gandhi: Father of a Nation*, 78.

3. Webb Miller, "Natives Beaten Down by Police in India Salt Bed Raid," United Press, May 21, 1930, http://100years.upi.com/sta_1930-05-21.html.

4. Denis Judd, *The Lion and the Tiger: The Rise and Fall of the British Raj* (Oxford, Eng.: Oxford University Press, 2004), 139.

5. Auroras Voice, "Season for Nonviolence 2012: March 5," http://aurorasvoice.org/index. php?option=com_content&view=ar ticle&id=84:season-for-nonviolence-2012&catid=4:news-archive&Itemid=9.

6. Downing, *Mohandas Gandhi*, 44.

7. Clément and Sharman, *Gandhi: Father of a Nation*, 86.

8. *Ibid.*, 98.

Decision Time
(pages 28–33)

1. Judd, *The Lion and the Tiger*, 152.

2. Clément and Sharman, *Gandhi: Father of a Nation*, 95.

3. Hatt, *Mahatma Gandhi*, 37.

4. *World Book Encyclopedia*, "India."

5. Judd, *The Lion and the Tiger*, 159.

6. Patrick French, *Liberty or Death: India's Journey to Independence* (London: HarperCollins, 1997), 154.

7. *Ibid.*, 154.

The Impact of Quit India
(pages 34–41)

1. Clément and Sharman, *Gandhi: Father of a Nation*, 96.

2. Finding Dulcinea, "On This Day: Gandhi's Arrest Sparks 'Quit India' Movement," August 9, 2011, http:// www.findingdulcinea.com/news/on-this-day/July-August-08/On-this-Day--Gandhi-s-Arrest-Launches-the-Quit-India-Movement.html.

3. French, *Liberty or Death*, 161.

4. B. R. Nanda, *Mahatma Gandhi: A Biography* (London: Unwin, 1965), 231.

5. *Ibid.*, 231.

6. Gandhian Institute Bombay and Gandhi Research Foundation, "Selected Writings of Mahatma Gandhi, Correspondence Between Mahatma Gandhi and Lord Linlithgow, Viceroy of India," http://www.mkgandhi.org/swmgandhi/chap08.htm.

7. James, *Raj*, 572.

8. *Ibid.*

9. *World Book Encyclopedia*, "India."

10. *Encyclopædia Britannica*, "India: Indian Nationalism and the British Response, 1885–1947," http://library.eb.co.uk/eb/article-214193.

Independence and Partition
(pages 42–49)

1. *Encyclopædia Britannica*, "India: Indian Nationalism and the British Response, 1885–1947."

2. D. R. SarDesai, I*ndia: The Definitive History* (Boulder: Westview Press, 2008), 309–313.

3. Catherine Clément and Ruth Sharman, *Gandhi: Father of a Nation*, 105.

4. Modern History Sourcebook, "Jawaharlal Nehru (1889-1964): Speech On the Granting of Indian Independence, August 14, 1947," http://www.fordham.edu/halsall/mod/1947nehru1.html.

5. Christine Hatt, *Mahatma Gandhi*, 53.

6. Downing, *Mohandas Gandhi*, 50.

7. Fordham University, "Modern History Sourcebook: Jawaharlal Nehru (1889–1964): Speech On the Granting of Indian Independence, August 14, 1947," http://www.fordham.edu/halsall/mod/1947nehru1.html.

8. GandhiServe Foundation, "Einstein on Gandhi," http://www.gandhiserve.org/streams/einstein.html.

9. Md. AnwarulIslam, "Freedom at Midnight," University of Dhaka, Bangladesh, Academia.edu, http://univdhaka.academia.edu/MdAnwarulIslam/Books/.../Freedom_at_midnight.

10. *Ibid.*

11. Downing, *Mohandas Gandhi*, 53.

What if...?
[pages 50–51]

1. Clément and Sharman, *Gandhi: Father of a Nation*, 91.

2. International Committee of the Red Cross, "The ICRC's Activities on the Indian Subcontinent Following Partition (1947–1949)," http://www.icrc.org/eng/resources/documents/misc/57jpcb.htm.

Gandhi's Legacy
[pages 52–53]

1. Clément and Sharman, *Gandhi: Father of a Nation*, 123.

2. French, *Liberty or Death*, 154.

3. Gandhian Institute Bombay and Gandhi Research Foundation, "Relevance of Gandhi, Champions of Non-violence," http://www.mkgandhi.org/articles/champions.htm.

Glossary

ahimsa doctrine of nonviolence, originally from the religion Jainism

All-India Muslim League also referred to as the Muslim League, this was an Indian political party to support Muslim interests

ally country or person who has agreed to help another

ashram religious community

Boer South African descended from Dutch settlers

boycott form of protest that involves not buying certain goods

British Empire empire of the United Kingdom

British India term for India when it was a colony of the United Kingdom

caste social class in Hindu society. There are traditionally four main castes: Brahmins (priests), Kshatriyas (soldiers), Vaishyas (merchants), and Shudras (farmers).

civil disobedience form of protest that may involve not paying taxes or not obeying certain laws

civil service body of government employees who run a country

civil war war within a country

colony country that is controlled by another

commonwealth association of states

democracy form of government in which people vote for representatives to govern them

diwan prime minister who governed on behalf of a prince in one of India's independent states

dominion country with self-government within the British Empire

export to send goods for sale abroad

extremist person with extreme political views

fascism form of government in which a country is led by a dictator

fast to choose not to eat

Hindi official language of India

Hindu follower of the Hindu religion

home rule self-government

hygiene cleanliness

import to bring goods into a country

Indian National Congress (INC) Indian political party which formed in the 1880s and later worked for Indian independence

Islamic belonging to Islam, the Muslim religion

legacy something that is handed down from one person to another

massacre mass killing of people or animals

morale confidence, good spirits

Muslim follower of Islam

Muslim League see All-India Muslim League

nationalist someone who is working to advance his or her country

noncooperation in India, a form of protest involving refusal to work with the UK administration

parliament elected government of a country

partition division; in Indian history, the term refers to the division of British India into India and Pakistan in 1947

plantation large farm or estate

prime minister title given to the chief minister in some democratic countries

princely state independent Indian state ruled by a prince

Raj UK rule in India

reconcile to come to an agreement

refugee someone who seeks shelter from persecution

satyagraha meaning "force of truth," it is a form of protest invented by Gandhi. The word comes from *satya* (truth) and *agraha* (force).

secular not relating to religion

separate electorates when members of a minority community vote only in seats set aside for their community, rather than voting for candidates in all seats

Sikh follower of the Sikh religion

Soviet Union union of communist states under Russia, which lasted from 1922 until 1991

subcontinent part of a continent, traditionally used to refer to India under the Raj

Untouchable member of the underclass of Hindu society, who do the dirtiest jobs

viceroy representative of the UK monarch in India; the highest official in India under the Raj

find Out More

Books

Downing, David. *Martin Luther King Jr. (Leading Lives)*. Chicago: Heinemann Library, 2002.

Downing, David. *Mohandas Gandhi (Leading Lives)*. Chicago: Heinemann Library, 2002.

Hatt, Christine. *Mahatma Gandhi (Judge for Yourself)*. Milwaukee: World Almanac Library, 2004.

For older readers

Gandhi, Mohandas. *An Autobiography or the Story of My Experiments with Truth*. Boston: Beacon, 2003 (originally published 1949).

Gandhi, Rajmohan. *Gandhi: The Man, His People, and the Empire*. Berkeley: University of California Press, 2008.

James, Lawrence. *Raj: The Making and Unmaking of British India*. New York: St. Martin's Griffin, 2000.

Judd, Denis. *The Lion and the Tiger: The Rise and Fall of the British Raj*. New York: Oxford University Press, 2004.

DVD

Gandhi (Sony Pictures Entertainment, 2007; first released 1982)
This award-winning movie, directed by Richard Attenborough, tells the story of Gandhi.

Web sites

www.gandhifoundation.net
Learn more about Gandhi at the web site of the Gandhi Research Foundation.

www.indianchild.com/history_of_india.htm
This site offers a comprehensive history of India.

www.mahatma.com
This web site is devoted to Gandhi's ideas, life, and times.

www.mkgandhi.org
This web site provides details about Gandhi's life and philosophy.

Other topics to research

Do research to learn more about topics related to the book. The following are some ideas to get you started:

- Discover more about non-violent campaigns and campaigners such as Martin Luther King Jr., the Dalai Lama, Aung San Suu Kyi, and Nelson Mandela. You could use "Champions of Non-violence," at www.mkgandhi.org/articles/champions.htm, as a starting point.

- Find out more about World War II, its causes, the progress of the war, and its outcome.

- Learn more about India under the British Raj.

Index